*Volume 71 of the Yale Series of Younger Poets*

CAROLYN FORCHÉ

# Gathering the Tribes

FOREWORD BY STANLEY KUNITZ

*Yale University Press*
*New Haven and London*
*1976*

Published with assistance from
The Mary Cady Tew Memorial Fund.

Library of Congress catalog card number: 75-32672
International standard book number: 0-300-01983-1 (cloth)
    0-300-01985-8 (paper)

Designed by Sally Sullivan
and set in Monotype Bembo type.
Printed in the United States of America by
Michael Bixler, Somerville, Massachusetts.

Published in Great Britain, Europe, and Africa by
Yale University Press, Ltd., London.
Distributed in Latin America by Kaiman & Polon,
Inc., New York City; in Australasia by Book & Film
Services, Artarmon, N.S.W., Australia;
in Japan by John Weatherhill, Inc., Tokyo.

*for my parents
and grandparents*

# Contents

*The Place That Is Feared I Inhabit*

# Acknowledgments

Acknowledgment is made to the following publications
for poems that originally appeared in them:

*Antaeus:* "Kalaloch," "Taking Off My Clothes"

*Chicago Review:* "Burning the Tomato Worms"

*Dacotah Territory:* "Ha Chi Je Na   I am Coming,"
    "Mientras Dure Vida, Sobra el Tiempo"

*Ms.:* "This Is Their Fault"

*Penny Dreadful:* "White Wings They Never Grow
    Weary"

*Quarry:* "Plain Song"

*Tugboat:* "Early Night," "What It Cost"

Thanks to the Helene B. Wurlitzer Foundation for their
assistance and Philip F. O'Connor for his help.

# Foreword

Kinship is the theme that preoccupies Carolyn Forché.
Although she belongs to a generation that is reputed to be
rootless and disaffiliated, you would never guess it from
reading her poems. Her imagination, animated by a gen-
erous life-force, is at once passionate and tribal. Narrative
is her preferred mode, leavened by meditation. She re-
members her childhood in rural Michigan, evokes her
Slovak ancestors, immerses herself in the American Indian
culture of the Southwest, explores the mysteries of flesh,
tries to understand the bonds of family, race, and sex. In
the course of her adventures she dares to confront, as a
sentient being, the overwhelming questions by which
reason itself is confounded: Who am I? Why am I here?
Where am I going?

In "Burning the Tomato Worms," a central poem, the
narrative focuses on Anna, "heavy sweatered winter
woman" seen "in horse-breath weather." She was the
poet's paternal grandmother, who spoke a Slovak of the
Russian-Czech borderlands and who, with her Old World
lore and old wives' tales, profoundly influenced the poet's
childhood.

> Anna's hands were like wheat rolls
> Shelling snow peas, Anna's hands
> Are both dead, they were Uzbek,
> Uzbek hands known for weaving fine rugs
>
> Eat Bread and Salt and Speak the Truth

Here as elsewhere the local color is vivid and unforced.
But the poem is not to be construed as an exercise in sen-

timentality or ethnic nostalgia: it is woven of two strands, one commemorating a beloved person and place, the other recounting a girl's sexual initiation. The burning of the tomato worms can be read as a ritual of purification. Everywhere in these pages ritual and litany are close at hand. Even the act of bread making, a recurrent image, assumes a ceremonial aspect.

*Love of people, love of place.* Carolyn Forché's poems give an illusion of artlessness because they spring from the simplest and deepest human feelings, from an earthling's awareness of the systemic pulse of creation. The poems tell us she is at home anyplace under the stars, wherever there are fields or mountains, lakes or rivers, persons who stir her atavistic bond-sense. In "Song Coming Toward Us" she writes:

> I am spirit entering
> the stomach of the stones.
>
> Bowls of clay and water sing,
> set on the fires to dry.
> The mountain moves
> like the spirit of southeast morning.
>
> You walk where drums are buried.
> Feel their skins tapping all night.
> Snow flutes swell ahead of your life.
> Listen to yourself.

She listens. At Justin Morrill College, an experimental residential branch of Michigan State University, where five years ago the earliest parts of *Gathering the Tribes* were conceived, she began her avid consumption of languages. Now she studies Russian, Spanish, Serbo-Croatian, French and Tewa (Pueblo Indian), listening beyond grammar for the secret texts. She acknowledges a primal sense of the power of words. The power to "make words"—in the mouth, in the heart, on the page—is the same to her as to give substance. Aiming at wholeness, strength, and clarity, she works at language as if it were a lump of clay or dough in her hands. In her search for poetry, in her effort to understand it, she has bent over the potter's wheel, climbed mountain ranges, ventured into the Mojave Desert. And she has sought out teachers. Among her teachers she lists her grandmother Anna, who died in 1968 ("Grandma, come back, I forgot/How much lard for these rolls"); her father, Michael Sidlosky, a tool and die maker, and her mother, Louise, who bore seven children before going to college, from which she graduated the same year as Carolyn, her eldest daughter; Teles Goodmorning of the Taos pueblo ("His voice scoops a swarm of coals,/dust rising from it"); Rosita of the same pueblo ("Her laugh is a music/from the time of Christ"); and Lama Kalu Rimpoche (an unknown and humble, very old man encountered in the mountains of New Mexico).

The places dearest to her include the south Michigan heartland where she was raised, Truchas and the Pueblo village of Taos in New Mexico, the Washington coast, and the Okanogan region of southern British Columbia. Anna, Alfansa, Teles Goodmorning, the dulcimer maker, Rosita, Jacynthe, the child born in the Okanogan, the monks of the mountain abbey, and Joey, a first love, who went off to study for the priesthood, are all characters clearly drawn from life and attached to specific locations. One might say that they are embodiments of the reality of their settings.

If I am right in supposing that "Year at Mudstraw," "Taking Off My Clothes," and "Kalaloch" are among the last poems written for this book, it would appear that Forché is moving toward a tauter line, packed with incisive detail, and a firmer dramatic structure than is evident in her earlier narratives. "Taking Off My Clothes" begins

> I take off my shirt, I show you.
> I shaved the hair out under my arms.
> I roll up my pants, I scraped off the hair
> on my legs with a knife, getting white.
>
> My hair is the color of chopped maples.
> My eyes dark as beans cooked in the south.
> (Coal fields in the moon on torn-up hills)

I have little doubt that the poem in *Gathering the Tribes* that will be most discussed, quoted, and anthologized is "Kalaloch" (pronounced ka-lā´-lok), an almost faultlessly controlled erotic narrative of 101 lines. In its boldness and innocence and tender, sensuous delight it may very well prove to be the outstanding Sapphic poem of an era. Here is its concluding section:

> Flies crawled us,
> Jacynthe crawled.
> With her palms she
> spread my calves, she
> moved my heels from each other.
> A woman's mouth is
> not different, sand moved
> wild beneath me, her long
> hair wiped my legs, with women
> there is sucking, the water
> slops our bodies. We come

clean, our clits beat like
twins to the loons rising up.

We are awake.
Snails sprinkle our gulps.
Fish die in our grips, there is
sand in the anus of dancing.
Tatoosh Island
hardens in the distance.
We see its empty stones
sticking out of the sea again.
Jacynthe holds tinder
under fire to cook the night's wood.

*If we had men 1 would make*
*milk in me simply*. She is
quiet. *I like that you*
*cover your teeth*.

Stanley Kunitz

*Burning the Tomato Worms*

# The Morning Baking

Grandma, come back, I forgot
How much lard for these rolls

Think you can put yourself in the ground
Like plain potatoes and grow in Ohio?
I am damn sick of getting fat like you

Think you can lie through your Slovak?
Tell filthy stories about the blood sausage?
Pish-pish nights at the virgin in Detroit?

I blame your raising me up for my Slav tongue
You beat me up out back, taught me to dance

I'll tell you I don't remember any kind of bread
Your wavy loaves of flesh
Stink through my sleep
The stars on your silk robes

But I'm glad I'll look when I'm old
Like a gypsy dusha hauling milk

# Burning the Tomato Worms

*That from which these things are born*
*That by which they live*
*That to which they return at death*
*Try to know that*

1

Now pines lift
Linking their dark spines
Weak clouds fly the breaks like pelicans
                              over ploughed land

During thick fields of American wind
Between apples and the first snow
In horse-breath weather I remember her

2

Before I was born, my body as snowfat
Crept over Wakhan
As grandfathers spat into fires and thawed
Their tarpaulin
Sending crackled paths of blood
Down into my birth

Their few logs were sleeves of fire
Twists of smoke still brush
Out of the ice where they died

3

Anna's hands were like wheat rolls
Shelling snow peas, Anna's hands
Are both dead, they were Uzbek,
Uzbek hands known for weaving fine rugs

Eat Bread and Salt and Speak the Truth

She was asking me to go with her
To the confrontation of something
That was sacred and eternal
It was a timeless, timeless thing
Nothing of her old age or my childhood
Came between us


4

Her footsteps bloodied snow
Smoke from her bread fire crept
From the house
The wood grew white in her stove

*When time come*
*We go quick*
*I think*
*What to take*

On her back ground wheat and straw dolls
In the sack white cheese, duck blood

*Mother of God*
*I tell you this*
*Dushenka*
*You work your life*
*You have nothing*


5

I came down from her in south Michigan
Picture the resemblance

Now I squint out over the same fields scraped in sun
And now I burn tomato worms and string useless gourds

She had drawn apple skin
Tightly bent feet
Pulled babushkas and rosary beads
On which she paid for all of us

She knew how much grease
How deep to seed
That cukes were crawlers

Every morning at five she would market
Or wake me to pick and hoe, crows
Cackling between us, Slovakia swear words
Whenever I stopped to feed them

This is the way we have it
Light a glass of candles
Heavy sweatered winter woman
Buried the October before I was grown


6

She would take gladiolas to the priest
Like sword sprouts they fumed near her bed

After raising my father and nine others
In a foreign country
*Find yourself a good man*
*Get married*
*There is nothing left*

*Before we have a village*
*Across the Slovakian border*
*Now*
*There is no Slovakia*

*Before we dance like gypsies*
*Listen*
*You—young yet*

## 7

Still the china Virgin
Plugs in below the mantelpiece, lights up
Pointing at her own heart
Big as a fist and full of daggers

I get down on my knees with every other Slavic woman
And we speak the language

## 8

She took up against her hoe stick, watched the moon
She could hear snow touch chopped wood
Her room smelled of advent candles
Cake flour clung to her face

## 9

Between apples and first snow
In horse-breath weather
Birds shape the wind
Dogs chained to the ground
Leave their dung
Where the ditches have burned

And I wish she were alive
But she is big under the ground, dead
I walk to the Eastern market
A half block under October suns that move away
Women still there selling summer squash
But always more die

## 10

Moons fill with blood nights
Crab-walking northeast
My father has left the garden
To seed, first frost
We lug tomatoes in worms and all

## 11

Stiff air, same color as a child's vein
Rigid against the freezing curls of birch bark
The snow's round thaw at fence-post bases
Snow deep across the yard
Ice grunting with boot heels
And a small sun an inch across like blood
On the frost when some trap
Chomps down a rabbit whose dark eyes
Wait for dogs

## 12

I chew up my gloves on the way to the barn
I wait in the pony stall for a boy
To come, circle his tongue
In my mouth while the stud horse
Muds floorboards beside us

Bales of feed split beneath
Our bellies, we wait like nothing
For tires to grind past beside us
Over a new fall in the road

All day snapping knives to the back side of the shed
He waits for me
Winter light spreading out in our houses
His own father downing a shot of Four Roses
Playing songs on combs and kleenex

*When you hear them hoot owls hollerin'*
*It's a sign a rain*

## 13

*I want to ask you why I live*
And we go back apart across the field
*Why I am here and will have to feel the way I die*

It was all over my face
Grandma flipped kolačy rolls
Dunked her hands in bowls of water
Looked at me
Wrung the rags into the stoop
Kept it from me
Whatever she saw

# What It Cost

In the pink tintype earliest hours,
we were moved out of Kiev.
Grey pelts to our necks smelling
as cold as in Wakhan on the dunged straw.
Asleep with fog in our mouths.

We ate the chunks bobbing in soup,
someone thinking it excrement, and drank
bad vodka poured over black breads.

Each slept where he sat, one window
in the whole place, beyond that
muslin snow mounded where
feed piles were left.

We each thought we knew someone
still alive who would butcher dogs
to cook.
This friend's name runs in damp sweat
until it bleeds enough, cannot be read.

We were young,
the children ate flesh
pulled from pyres.
Mothers wrapped dead babies
in blankets and carried them.

As we will never know what it means,
we will know what it cost.

Our icons, our cross, balalaikas
burning up.
Goose down, wagons full of tarps
and crockery and deaths
throughout the tundra, deaths
as the trains steamed through snow
into sunrise.

We never stopped at towns.
Old blue hands in snowbanks
motioned on:

*Haul your language south.*
*There are knives in your pillows.*
*The white birds fall another month.*

# Early Night

I wrap myself in sheep leather,
kick heavy snow over its own tough skin.
Snow, daylight, ghosts in my mouth.

Here my round Slovak face feels like
whale meat on soapstone, I cannot
touch myself without screaming.
With a fist of Slavic I toss
old forgotten language to birds
asleep in flight, in snarling ice they stuff
their faces in their wings.

Hold to the wooden arms of bare oak.

I walk like this alone, old country
boots munching the field.
This snow is the snow of Urals
swarming upward, ashes, birds
frozen solid into stars.

# Barley Fields

There is a strange list
to the wet range of clouds
stroking our fields:
heavy pheasants were
high in the wind, high over
currant shrubs, unmown grain.

Old trees moan like a boat,
we call their branches witch arms.
They toss worn gloves at us
as if we are ready to be
shoveled over with dirt.

Pulling damp bedding
from clips, running
great straw baskets to the house.
Silver-bellied grasses lift
their cat fur, cold spit
blotching us, we hurry.
Veins of wind light up, we see
the color of its blood.

For an hour we lean on north walls,
wearing blankets, the house underwater.
We see ourselves circle through
streets, gripping shingles, we see ourselves
caught in the highest branches
rising from the water, fish claws.
But all this wind
hits the barley field and dies.

# Dulcimer Maker

Calf-deep in spruce dust,
wood curls off his knife,
blade wet, bare bulb light.

The finish of his hands
shows oil, grain, knots
where his growth scarred him.

Planing black oak
thin to flow sounds.
Tones of wind filling
bottle lips.

It is his work tying strings
across fresh-cut pine.

He sings into wood, listens:
tree rings, water!

The wood drinks his cloth,
its roots going to the depths of him,
spreading.

He wants to build a lute for music
carved on Sumerian stones, a music
no one has heard for three thousand years.

For this he will work
the oldest wood he can find.
It will not be as far away,
as unfamiliar.

# From Memory

The boar hog shovels his voice into mudslop
where corn rolls, stripped.
Come fall he will be cut: his hams,
pork links rocking in smoke.
Grandma sharpens her knife on Arkansas.
Sam bends, spits chew in the bucket,
the breeze quits.
Spiders tie nets to fruit jars,
it is boring with them in Blue Hills
when gum trees blossom.
Their thoughts are like dust in a salt box.
Boring pig blood perks below ground.

Their palsied hands like horse tails swishing flies.

*Song Coming Toward Us*

## Calling Down The Moose

Near lone pine
remote men
spit out chew.
Moose lope
unbroken snows,
their branches scooping
the creak of the woods.
With their toes they
melt the fields.

> *Everything happens*
> *in the same space.*
> *What has been*
> *and what is becoming*
> *are all of the same age.*

The days here draw on
like a rockful of sun.
Quiet paw holes of a herd
in the fall and men quiet
because of their lives
call down moose
from the mountain.

# Song Coming Toward Us

I am spirit entering
the stomach of the stones.

Bowls of clay and water sing,
set on the fires to dry.
The mountain moves
like the spirit of southeast morning.

You walk where drums are buried.
Feel their skins tapping all night.
Snow flutes swell ahead of your life.
Listen to yourself.

I am spirit living
thin wooden years
around the aspen.

You live
like a brief wisp
in a giant place.

## Blue Mesa

A cottonwood surfaces in the reservoir.
It uproots itself with the breath it has held
since the river rose over the woods.
It rolls with life in the slap of waters.

Trout swim between pines, the fly fisher
whips the lake and the lines
dropped from barely moving boats
tie men to the calm spring canyon.

## Skin Canoes

Swallows carve lake wind,
trailers lined up, fish tins.
The fires of a thousand small camps
spilled on a hillside.

I pull leeks, morels from the soil,
fry chubs from the lake in moonlight.
I hear someone, hear the splash, groan
of a waterpump, wipe my mouth.
Fish grease spits at darkness.

Once I nudged a canoe through that water,
letting its paddle lift, drip.
I was sucked down smaller than the sound
of the dropping, looked out
from where I had vanished.

# Ha Chi Je Na    I Am Coming

*for Firelin*

Near Tonasket
in the Okanogan hills
at red moon,
there was a fire
stirred, whipped, steady
in apple wood.

The darkness swelled
as clouds crossed, blended
the night.

A tipi smoked in the aspen clearing.
A hoot owl's head swirled.
This gave us time.

One went out and padded through marsh for yarrow.
He sat down and peeled it for sticks to be thrown.
One leaned on a scrub pine shaking within himself.
Inside the tipi his wife's breath chanted.

Not far
from the Havillah route
Jupiter lighted
a quiet road.

In the aspen clearing
her water broke,
yarrow came clean:

Thunder within the earth.
The image of the turning point.
The owl.

The brook ran pink until
out pots were full to set
on the fire.
The lake it fed
cracked, scattered.
Flames rubbed iron,
set water loose.

We had something to do
while she cried, no blame.

She bit a strap as sky
fainted, even before
burns showed near the east edge,
before light scratched the mountains,
one moved
away from her, one slid
to the blanket through her blood.

We roasted the birth sac
on coals and each ate some.
The first milk flowed.

# Mountain Abbey, Surrounded by Elk Horns

Bells crack ice, white cattle
chew clean
red slopes that back away
from the mountain monastery.

Seventeen years of solitude is seventeen
years. Quiet. Punching eighty loaves of bread
a day, delivering
small cows.

Dawns thin out, like onion leaves,
each day's reading,
such pale paper
that it fills an open window.

Knowing dry feet of birds,
small sky between summits,
the swelling of animal mothers.

Each day, relived, a matter
of faith
that white cattle biting
sage of this hillside were not
already slaughtered.

# Goodmorning and the White Girl

Ya-Kwana
in her kitchen cutting
a dead pig into steaks,
a box of black hair dye
near her, the boarded horno
where her breads have been
the winter.

She smiles horsebeans.
With sleeves of fat she
works, she laughs until
there are crows in the room,
crows!
The crease this water pail has worn
in her palm, what will
that line mean to her life?
Her skirt splashed with slop marks of water.

*Um-pee-eh-na-mo?* I have come to say
good-bye to Teles Goodmorning, grandpa.
She points me behind the blanket.
He is there, Tiem-goo, Goodmorning, Teles
Reyna to the Spanish people.
His hands in the fogon making
fire, hot wood swimming up his arms.
eighty-three this April, he has told me, this time
his years will be almost enough.

I will be planting hawk wings
on the mound of dirt above him.
*Um-pee-eh-na-mo.* Rattle of
loose teeth, tough snow, Ya-
Kwana in the other room.

The fire tongues cluck, tisk
in the bark, Tewa shaking in his mouth
like oats, sticks, the words.
He holds
a pie pan of cedar leaves,
they smoke: rolled Bugler, slow end of winter.

*Pa-ana, sa-ana, I will fill this empty*
*gourd with stones, tie snowbird*
*feathers in buckskin, bead a stick.*
*I will tie up perfume leaves*
*and send you to Ohio with pey-yo.*
*You will be okay where they grow tomatoes.*

His voice scoops a swarm of coals,
dust rising from it.
There is nothing more, the stars
bunched like a herd of goats above
his house, the dogs
yapping from the road, hanging
their yipes from trees.

## Las Truchas

Adobe walls crack, rot in Las Truchas.
Sometimes a child in a doorway
or dog stretched on the road.
Always a quiet place.
Wooden wheelbarrows rest up against
boarded windows.
Not yet Semana Santa
when people of Truchas and Mora
will fill them with human bones
and walk with blood-stained eyes
in the mountains where Pecos water
flows among cork-barked fir
and foxtail grows dwarfed, gnarled.

Strangers who drive the high road
to Taos pass through Truchas.
They buy Cordova's rugs and weavings,
hear the wooden flute of the hermit.
Their minds drift to sleep in thin sky.
They hear stories about Penitentes,
that they crucify each other, whip themselves
at night screaming names of God.
Yet they return to Truchas to build
brick homes like wagons circling.
Ptarmigans fly in pines singing nothing.

Every year the village is more quiet.
The creak of wheels, whispers.
No, it is nothing.
But the village seems empty
while the smoke still winds
from sun-baked homes and the people
bless the snow.

# Alfansa

*My spirit is a wafer of smoke*
*rising from a source snapping in silence*
*a sound of something old, dry, ready to be burned.*

I

Alfansa strings Chimayo's chilis,
like sacred hearts, tongues of fire tied together.
Hollow, rattling chili seed, glowing from
within like wax lamps.

Chimayo's homes are blood-colored earth,
washing from streams that claw down
Sangre de Christos.
Cottonwoods shiver dust,
from handfuls of mud, from wood beams,
men of Chimayo, Cundiyo built the mission.
People come to this Santuario,
smear themselves with mud, light candles.
Lift dry mud from the mud well to their mouths.
(It fills by itself while they sleep.)

Earth is carried off in clothes of cripples
weeping 'el posito, jesu, christu.'
They bring baby shoes to the statue
of the Child, its shoes wear soft, thin
while the hole is filling.
Their crutches they
string on Santuario's walls.

2

She was born Chimayo, deer
cried below highmilk.
As a child her father roamed San Mateo.
She, color of clays, worked quietly.

In the mud house, Jorge, Pasha, she
washed flies from their faces, wrung wash, dreamed
of damp nights, slit windpipes of beef.

Young, believing clay spirits, black winds
tunneled to her sleep.
Madre de Dios, she heard Maria whisper
in yellow pine '*alfansa*.'

### 3

When she was eighty, her neck
swelled, lack of salt.
Like a sack of worms
crawling there, sometimes
a sandbag tied on her voice.
She lived with it, held it
when she spoke as if it would
drop from her throat.
She heard a voice of hills '*alfansa*.'

It told her the secret
not only of Cundiyo, but Mora, beyond.

### 4

Beads drip from their fists in Santuario,
between each decade men sing like Hebrews.
Voices as clean as pine root boiled in fire.
Alfansa covers her hair, goes to the mission
alone at night in emptiness.
Dust covers Christ, Alfansa
wipes Him, hauls baskets of soil
to the well weeping '*posito, jesu*,'
rubbing shoes on her lips.

Snow stains Sangre de Christos
faintly the color of wounds.

5

Morning. People come
to this hole that fills itself,
reaching down to touch
new growths of the earth.

All the while Alfansa pounds corn, her goiter
growing hot pulp like Chimayo chili, Hail Marys, worry
for her husband who is dead.

# Tortugas

*You will know someone for many years.*
*He will not speak to you of this until*
*it's time.*

Women wrap in rebosas, men
in dark cloth.
They light stub torches, these
rocking high in their arms to each house.
Throughout Tortugas, speechless circles
move close enough to fires in snow to be burned.

They carry the statue through doorways.
Families gather before it, murmur
of deaths, scoops of corn, dust of grains
poured from their summer.
They tell who has gone to fight, what
happened.
Simply, snow, silent faces.

You will go to Tortugas as I did, your flesh
turned to breath in Christos, your blood
will surface when you hear these voices,
this news, these people, their bells, your skin
comes to touch this fire.

Don't touch it.
Don't ask them why they walk, why at
Christmas in Tortugas this happens.
Don't live on their land, it was taken away
in your lifetime.
But go to Tortugas in the month when earth
swells, while it sleeps, before seas of snow
slide off like flesh shed in fire.

# Mientras Dure Vida, Sobra el Tiempo

*Memory becomes very deep, weighs more, moves less.*

### 1

She is a good woman, walking
in the body of a twisted bush, as old
as the ones who are gone.
Her teeth, chips of winter river
thawed, swallowed
or spit out.

On the way to town her hands
fly in and out her shawl
catching scraps of her voice,
feathers fallen from birds.
Like mud hens, her hands.

She buys coffee, medicine, pork.
Squats on the grocery floor
digging in her breasts
for money.
She is no higher than chamisa
or wild plum trees
grown for more than a hundred years
beside the river.

### 2

I feel the mountains moving
closer, with smoke
on their faces, hear cries
in couloirs of snow.

Last night a woman not alive
came to my bedside, a black skirt, black

reboso. She touched
my blankets, sang like wind
in a crack, saw
that my eyes were open.
She went to the kitchen
without footsteps,
rattled pans, sang *ma-he-yo*

*Ma-he-yo* until morning.


### 3

On the way from town Rosita
leads me through rosy dust of North Plaza.
My face shrivels, I shrink through her
doorway.

On her walls, a washtub, Jesus.
One room.
La yerba del manso tied,
hung from a nail to dry.
Green chili, a blanket
dyed to match the field.
She has lived alone.


### 4

Rosita kneeling at her fogon,
since morning no fire.
Wind bony, dark as her face
when at night she holds
her eyes in her hands.

She stacks stumps of piñon,
lights a match.
I drop like piñon at her feet.
Fire rushes from her hands, her hands

flutter, flames, her bones
shine like tongs through her flesh.

Sparks on the ground turning into women
who begged to be let go, that night
on the llano.
People talk, people tell
these stories.
People say "leave Rosita alone or you are
malificiada."
Her laugh is a music
from the time of Christ.
Rosita's eyes shatter
la tristeza de la vida,
dog-stars within them.

*You, you live alone*
*in your life.*
*Your life will have ma-he-yo.*
*I never married, never*
*cut my hair.*
*Ma-he-yo are blessings of God.*
*That is all the English I have.*


5

On another day she disappeared,
her door open, her eyes
seen in the face of a dog
near the river.

*You will light fires*
*with one touch.*
*You will make one death*
*into another.*

# Ancapagari

In the morning of the tribe this name Ancapagari was given to these mountains. The name, then alive, spread into the world and never returned. Ancapagari: no footstep ever spoken, no mule deer killed from its foothold, left for dead. Ancapagari opened the stones. Pine roots gripped peak rock with their claws. Water dug into the earth and vanished, boiling up again in another place. The water was bitten by aspen, generations of aspen shot their light colored trunks into space. Ancapagari. At that time, if the whisper was in your mouth, you were lighted.

Now these people are buried. The root-taking, finished. Buried in everything, thousands taken root. The roots swell, nesting. Openings widen for the roots to surface.

They sway within you in steady wind of your breath. You are forever swinging between this being and another, one being and another. There is a word for it crawling in your mouth each night. Speak it.

Ancapagari has circled, returned to these highlands. The yellow pines deathless, the sparrow hawks scull, the waters are going numb. Ancapagari longs to be spoken in each tongue. It is the name of the god who has come from among us.

## Plain Song

When it happens, let the birds come.
Let my hands fall without being folded.
And naked in hair that grows on the dead,
tie feathers from the young female.

Close my eyes with coins, cover
my head with agave baskets
that have carried water.

Bring the tub drums and dance.
Bring me to burn with a mesquite branch
and wear the bones that I leave
around your necks.

*The Place That Is Feared I Inhabit*

# The Place That Is Feared I Inhabit

*for Falling Rock*

I

Sun dropped behind Castle Rocks until the man and woman, some distance from each other, went dark, blending with jasper ledges and brilliance of clay bluffs in late light. Ice coated junipers, turned their berries to stone, brought wren song up from the branches. Other than this, no sound, wind swallowing the ground. Wind swirling its massive thoughts through dry weeds, bleached wood of drained mesquite, man-forms of joshua. A coyote moved on blood-colored sky, head bowed to dust. Later its black lips round as a flute. It darkened. Stars cracked, burning in the various distance. Then as if no man had ever lived, the earth breathed from its stones a fine, ground dust. As if only hunting birds moved, cleaned the sky, flew at the moon, watched the ground breathe. The creator smoothed over the valley. The man and woman were quiet and their thoughts passed between them. These were of the substance of motionless wind, awake to the quiet, quiet within the hungry space of their presence.

## II

Hides of snow had begun to shrink
from the mountains, hides
from the bones of cows, she comes
upon flesh half-eaten, Taloache, moon.

Clutching Hualapais face-rock,
her body packed rope, her mouth
smeared in bird blood, it dries
up her arms.

When ghost town planks pop
in her fire, she sees his face
on her thigh.

He was reverent, running
palm-wood hands over walls
covered with writing:

*You are speaking to me.*
*I know you are a spirit.*
*I have finished my drum.*

The sun sits on far hills,
puffs dry clouds, wraps
in alpaca.
Two logs hug smoke, she kneels, this light.
Small winds lift coyotes, for miles
her horrified face lights their howls.

Hunger stars, dry slopes appear.
A broken flight hardens in her belly.
She smells that she's been rinsed in fire.

*There are many worlds, we go back to nothing.*
He said this and yet saw breath on the dead.
He taught that she moved from burial to burial.

He found veins of turquoise
slushing through solid hills.
He wore tobacco, rolled her
naked through the sun.

Before death she had taken
him in her mouth, now her tongue
shrivels old white songs.

She made her way from him,
from their truck, cold, broken.
She left him with an empty
gun in the open.

In the brush of a south rill
birds tear up his shirt.
She thinks the shard of flesh
dropped from a hawk's flight
was his.

They remain unburied in Sonora.
In bowls of stone
their ribs clutch mud.

# Taproot

In this gulch of San Juan
you toss boulders, through
highland silence they crack
like tough eggs.
I catch them in my arms
like a peasant, *mokva*,
carry them across the water
to lay a floor for a fire.

The million winds dig
windows in the hills.
I hear the hollow crackle
of hatching snakes.

Kneecaps, lost skulls, stones
pound into the canyon like elk.

2

We slip an old Dodge
tailgate beneath the pots.
The iron swims, a stone lake.

Rhubarb boils down to its strings.
Water hissing in trout.

When we have eaten
we swallow lumped smoke of piñon.
A cloud of stars gathers as if
thoughts too distant for time will snow
this night.

I was eight, you, eleven,
when we agreed to meet here.


3

Our goat moths
tore themselves to shreds on your wall.
Your father curled your back
with his belt, a metal buckle ringing
on your spine like a small bell.

You killed some fish, took them
to the woodblock with knives,
pails of water.
I watched you from a distance
slitting their bellies,
pulling from them white combs.
You chased me with their hearts,
stomachs
wagging at the edge of your hands.
You were just as afraid.

You spent the day chopping grasses,
wheeling mulch.
While you hacked at the field
as if it were endless, I ran
with younger girls, a woman.


4

I am pretending to sleep with you:
the priest holding a swab of bread
over my hair.
You stand beside him with a gold
platter fluttering under my face.
I close my eyes, feel
a body on my tongue,
yours.

I am sleeping, we stagger
through snow, fire, you are half
dead, bones soaked through your skin.
We are hidden from whips in the night.

In the morning your roof
breathes peacefully.
Your father starts his car.
Your window was a dark
painting then
hanging in the stones of your house.

5

You write from Holy Cross Abbey:

Last night after vespers I was wandering.
One of the young monks thought he was alone.
I watched him cup the breasts of the hand-carved
virgin in his hands.
Meet me at Spring Creek.

6

Hawks ride from Finger Rock
hearing wild mice rustle at my feet.
You had matted a clearing, you were
stirring your fire when I saw you.
There had been no time between.

7

These are my breasts, your eyelids
on my throat, *are you hungry?*
You have cut stalks of rhubarb
from the water.
There are two nests of magpie,
a fresh run-off, elk

a thousand feet upland, I have seen them
trampling clouds until rain drummed here.

You seem quiet.

8

Your eyes are snowy,
a glass crèche, Christmas, I have
shaken your eyes.

You find a log for me to sit on.
You knew we would be old, in this fire
we watch ourselves play with each other.

Our mamas shielding their eyes from the sun.

## This Is Their Fault

A day moon, frozen in the front window before dawn. I pour coffee, toast bread, the bluish wind east. I waken the young ones, nudging quilt piles. Snow hovers, too light. Wool scarves tied across their mouths. They leave, they are all gone.

I turn out lights, watch broken sky raise off the ground and the air pale out. I fill the sink, start to clean, clearing plates, sweeping, cleaning. I smell the old garlic press in my hands, hold it underwater, standing at this same window scrubbing clove bits from the same press I washed when I was a young girl. The window, the hollow madonna on the sill, full of brillo pads, the same. The day will be brilliant, from a quiet Arizona dawn I saw once. I sprinkle dry yeast in scalded milk, lay the cup on the wiped shelf.

The house out back of us. Oil drum empty, ash can, sheet-plastic and masking-tape windows, tape flapping, shuffled. Nine young ones living there. I smear the dishrag along the drain board. Remember when I took care of them all, their mother fallen ill. I went to bake food in their house, found meal worms nosing through flour sacks, squirmy in the flower-print cloth. Human dung in the corners of the house, hard, balled up.

Splashing puffed corn with sweet-milk, holding to each a washed can of it. One of the smallest taking his penis out of his coveralls, holding it in his sticky palm, tickling it. Scrubbing meal off pots under the water trickle, well water rosy with iron, wondering how this happens. The bony young girls making kitchen curls with hairpins while I am thinking *this is their fault*, they won't clean themselves. The mama, thin, drunk, stares at the steam heater and her spit-up.

Joey's tree comes clear in the morning light, rotten, wood steps nailed to its sides, bare, crippled. A crow daubed to one branch, flapping through the rest. Joey gone to a monastery in Canada, keeping a vow. He grew up here, his wood steps he nailed to that tree and put it to death. A pearl communion rosary I had, mama strung it. Now the crow flies overland, somehow his flight is heavy.

Dry cracks of wood, chopped up, hauled in to warm off. I lift the saucer off the yeast batch. How much I wanted to marry him when I was eight, nine. The sun hard, the sudden decision of that starling to leave the phone line, wires so fine they finally vanish. I wanted him to chase me back of the woodpile, hold me by the hair. Make me lick his boots, show him my nipples, cry, feel the tingle in my pants that comes of that.

I spoon lard, let it drop and spread in hot milk, toss salt, finally whip the batter with a spoon, when mama's gone like this I can think. I can watch the field where Joey shot hay bales, where I'd watch him, find some reason to go outside. What did I want then? How I thought nights, some man with no face, then reach my hands down, grab my cunt by the bowlful, two small hands, flat body. Curtain filling, screen wide open. Dark, the mounds of quilt rising and falling, the bed squeaky and rocking. Working myself to sleep, knowing I should hide what I was doing, not knowing what it was. At first I had only to strip for him, he would make me ashamed. The crickets scraped legs together in the flowers. I was tied up, I was milked, beaten, I was sold, they stuck their fingers in me, twirling from a rope. Must do this or be ground like beef or fed to horses. The nights smelled of cow's breath. I'd roll off my hands and let the wind come dust me, shape the pillow into Joey's chest and sleep. I work the dough beneath my fists, pull it back toward me, punch it then dust it with flour again.

## Year at Mudstraw

Listen to the pine splits
crack in the stove.
Clouds down our roof like
burnt pine, milk.
The smell of come in the shack.

A breeze on the wall
from boiling tomatoes.
A baby snorts air
while it sucks me.

It was time to put apricots
out in the sun,
cover them with cheesecloth.

Nothing but the whine of bad mud
between the cabin logs.
I hum Cold Blew The Bliss
to the child, touch fattened dough.
I wait for the sound of his truck
hoeing a splutter of thawed ditch.

And when he comes he points his rifle
at the floor, lets the dog
smell his pants.

Soup's about done, my breasts
dropping from pot steam.
He slides a day's beard down my neck.
I open my clothes to his hands.

One buck in the woods, but too quick.
My nipples stiffen, his touch.
I want to swallow down his come,
something in his heart
freezes in a dead run.

# Taking Off My Clothes

I take off my shirt, I show you.
I shaved the hair out under my arms.
I roll up my pants, I scraped off the hair
on my legs with a knife, getting white.

My hair is the color of chopped maples.
My eyes dark as beans cooked in the south.
(Coal fields in the moon on torn-up hills)

Skin polished as a Ming bowl
showing its blood cracks, its age, I have hundreds
of names for the snow, for this, all of them quiet.

In the night I come to you and it seems a shame
to waste my deepest shudders on a wall of a man.

You recognize strangers,
think you lived through destruction.
You can't explain this night, my face, your memory.

You want to know what I know?
Your own hands are lying.

# Kalaloch

The bleached wood massed in bone piles,
we pulled it from dark beach and built
fire in a fenced clearing.
The posts' blunt stubs sank down,
they circled and were roofed by milled
lumber dragged at one time to the coast.
We slept there.

Each morning the minus tide—
weeds flowed it like hair swimming.
The starfish gripped rock, pastel,
rough. Fish bones lay in sun.

Each noon the milk fog sank
from cloud cover, came in
our clothes and held them
tighter on us. Sea stacks
stood and disappeared.
They came back when the sun
scrubbed out the inlet.

We went down to piles to get
mussels, I made my shirt
a bowl of mussel stones, carted
them to our grate where they smoked apart.
I pulled the mussel lip bodies out,
chewed their squeak.
We went up the path for fresh water, berries.
Hardly speaking, thinking.

During low tide we crossed
to the island, climbed

its wet summit. The redfoots
and pelicans dropped for fish.
Oclets so silent fell
toward water with linked feet.

Jacynthe said little.
Long since we had spoken *Nova Scotia,*
*Michigan,* and knew beauty in saying nothing.
She told me about her mother
who would come at them with bread knives then
stop herself, her face emptied.

I told her about me,
never lied. At night
at times the moon floated.
We sat with arms tight
watching flames spit, snap.
On stone and sand picking up
wood shaped like a body, like a gull.

I ran barefoot not only
on beach but harsh gravels
up through the woods.
I shit easy, covered my dropping.
Some nights, no fires, we watched
sea pucker and get stabbed
by the beacon
circling on Tatoosh.


   2

I stripped and spread
on the sea lip, stretched
to the slap of the foam
and the vast red dulce.
Jacynthe gripped the earth
in her fists, opened—

the boil of the tide
shuffled into her.

The beach revolved,
headlands behind us
put their pines in the sun.
Gulls turned a strong sky.
Their pained wings held,
they bit water quick, lifted.
Their looping eyes continually
measure the distance from us,
bare women who do not touch.

Rocks drowsed, holes
filled with suds from a distance.
A deep laugh bounced in my flesh
and sprayed her.

3

Flies crawled us,
Jacynthe crawled.
With her palms she
spread my calves, she
moved my heels from each other.
A woman's mouth is
not different, sand moved
wild beneath me, her long
hair wiped my legs, with women
there is sucking, the water
slops our bodies. We come
clean, our clits beat like
twins to the loons rising up.

We are awake.
Snails sprinkle our gulps.
Fish die in our grips, there is
sand in the anus of dancing.
Tatoosh Island
hardens in the distance.
We see its empty stones
sticking out of the sea again.
Jacynthe holds tinder
under fire to cook the night's wood.

*If we had men I would make
milk in me simply.* She is
quiet. *I like that you
cover your teeth.*

# White Wings They Never Grow Weary

*for Dara Wier*

Stars, crisp in the deep plot
pulling off, late snow clouds
clean themselves.
The river lets loose the carp,
coughs beneath its frozen part.

Drippings on the roof hit the gutter.
Ice branches ripped off in wind are waterborne.

In the house, a rim of cheese is quiet.
There is a chunk of lard to be rendered.
I should hang pails on the trees and wait for sugar.

I want to tie off the time like a birth cord
chewed broken in a proud woman's teeth.
My navel is gone, the moon up,
in a month or two my breasts will be in pain.
Out here a woman wonders.

And if she has no man her arms get strong.
When seasons change she can't believe
there will ever be milk in her body.

Ever believe there will be someone
asking something from her.